Latest 'Days Out' Hertfordshire fro[m] Albans

by The South Herts Transport User Group

1

South Herts Transport User Group

4

A brochure style booklet publication giving a varied guide to modern attractions and 'days out' by bus across Hertfordshire from St. Albans

Written and compiled by Paul Spelzini c/o the South Herts Transport user Group.

South Herts Transport User Group

South Herts Transport User Group

The bus is the key to a great day out. Offering great value for money (or free if you hold a concessionary pass!) we have suggested a range of places to visit whatever your age, interest, or the weather! Shopping, museums, walks, attractions, countryside, gardens, sport, historic towns, traditional tea rooms and even TV shows all feature! All the places listed are accessible by bus from Potters Bar, although may involve a change or two or travel by rail where there is no direct bus connection.

If you have a concessionary pass, it is valid on all the bus services but if you pay fares on the bus, you will probably find an Explorer ticket offers best value giving the freedom of virtually all buses in Hertfordshire and beyond. If there are two or more of you and you are staying together all day the Group Explorer offers you a great deal for £17 for up to four people. Buy your Explorer ticket from the driver of the first bus you board, Check travel information before starting a journey. We will do our best to keep this up to date, but we cannot be held responsible if bus services or attractions change at short notice. Please check the arrangements before travelling.

South Herts Transport User Group

Hertfordshire County Show

The highlight of the county year held at the Redbourn Showground every year over the bank holiday weekend in late May. Displays of agriculture, food, farming, livestock, and sheepdog displays, funfairs, games and have a go. Opportunity to try out different foodstuffs, brews, and drinks. Great fun for all the family. Tractor pulls, dog shows, ducks and geese, horses and sheep pens plus show rings and many other events.

Bus 34 to Redbourn Showground (Saturday) or taxi or Uber (Sunday).

De Havilland Aircraft Museum

Located at Salisbury Hall, London Colney opposite the M25, the museum was founded to preserve the legacy of the De-Havilland name. The de Havilland Aircraft Museum's mission is to preserve and communicate the de Havilland Heritage to ensure that current and future generations of all ages will understand de Havilland's contribution to innovative British Aviation technology. The de Havilland Aircraft Museum's volunteers are dedicated to restoring de-Havilland aircraft and artefacts. The New Hangar has provided additional facilities that has enabled more aircraft to be under cover and ensure that the restoration process can continue in all weathers as

15

well as providing visitors with the opportunity to enjoy practical and informative learning opportunities.

Bus 84 to London Colney

St. Albans and St. Michaels

The only city in Hertfordshire with historic roots dating back to Roman times, with Roman remains in Verulamium Park, Verulamium arena, the Abbey, roman walling, and artefacts in the local museums. An attractive shopping centre, but also has a regular Wednesday and Saturday and special Christmas and Easter markets selling all kinds of merchandise. The city holds regular festivals all year round and has one of the oldest pubs in England in the fighting cocks. Also has the picturesque Fishpool Street historic area and St. Michaels, sadly now with only one remaining pub but numerous cafes and restaurants and the delightful George Street with its antique shops, plus new museums.

South Herts Transport User Group

Bus 302 or S7 from St. Albans

Berkhamsted

Visit this historic market town situated on the Grand Union Canal with many interesting old buildings. The lively street market is held on Wednesdays and Saturdays and there is good and interesting range of shops, cafes, and pubs. It was here that in 1066 that William the Conqueror was offered the Crown of England. The beautiful ruins of Berkhamsted Castle are well worth a visit and have many stories to tell. Change to Arriva route 300/302 at St. Albans, every 15 minutes weekdays, 20 minutes Saturdays and hourly Sundays. Change to the 500 at Hemel; runs every 20 minutes Mondays to Fridays and every 30 mins Saturdays. On Sundays, the service runs every 60 mins (Red Rose 501).

Bus 302 to Hemel Hempstead then Bus 500 Weekdays/ 501 Sundays.

21

Harry Potter World, Leavesden

Change in St. Albans city centre then Watford Junction station to Mullaney's Buses 311 which takes you straight to the Warner Brothers studios and enjoy a day out at the fantastic Harry Potter World. Now the #1 visitor attraction in Hertfordshire. Average visit times are 3-4 hours. We will not spoil the surprises if you have never been yet. This is of interest to all and is an absolute must see for children and every lifelong Harry Potter fan and anyone who has seen any of the films. If you have been before, find out about the new exhibits since your last visit. Please note you must buy tickets in advance and the attraction may be closed at certain times so check before travelling.
https://www.wbstudiotour.co.uk/tickets.

Bus 321 or 724 to Watford Junction station, then Harry Potter World shuttle bus

South Herts Transport User Group

South Herts Transport User Group

Elstree Studios

You can become a member of the audience and watch one of your favourite TV shows being filmed – all for free. Shows such as Strictly Come Dancing, The Chase have been filmed at Elstree over the past year. Some shows such as Pointless are filmed daytimes. Sky plans a huge expansion here over the next few years to make this into a real international hub for TV and film creating thousands of new jobs.

Visit www.sroaudiences.com or www.applause.com

Bus 601 to Elstree weekdays

South Herts Transport User Group

John Lewis, Welwyn

One of Hertfordshire's oldest and original department stores. Spend a morning or afternoon exploring the full range of goods on show and shop both in the traditional and modern ways. Departments to cover all household needs and more specialised purchases. Have tea or lunch in the spacious cafeteria restaurant overlooking the green at Welwyn, one of Hertfordshire original new towns, with its classic lines. A landmark store in the garden city reflecting a bygone era and experience a different way of life once common in the early 20th century.

Bus 302

South Herts Transport User Group

Herts wood Forest and The Timberland Trail

A large swathe of forest and land reclaimed for leisure, walking and horse riding including some farmland stretching from Smallford village via London Colney, Shenley to Elstree and Borehamwood. Part of the Herts wood Forest project is to plant a million trees and rewild areas once used as disused gravel pits, streams, pasture, and reclaimed lakes. The Timberland Trail has been set up to allow walkers to take pre-planned walks through these areas that nature has reclaimed, with species of flora and fauna returning where once threatened. Sponsored by Timberland walking boots, with maps and brochures also available online.

Bus 305 (Small ford) or bus 84 then 602/357 (Shenley) or bus 601 (Borehamwood)

33

35

Upper Lea Valley and Northaw Great Wood

An area of outstanding natural beauty and often described as
one of the most scenic summer bus rides in the whole of the
UK, on the former London Country bus service 350, which
sadly no longer runs. However, you can enjoy walking the
footpaths and bridleways between Hertford castle and its weir,
and former LNER country stations at Hertingfordbury and Cole
Green. Visit country pubs at Essendon, and the Cowper Arms
at Cole Green for a hearty lunch and pint, plus villages with
pubs at Brickendon, Essendon Green, and Newgate Street,
etc. You can follow the trail of the Upper River Lea itself and
its varied wildlife in summer and enjoy the views and some of
the best Herts countryside between Hertford and Essendon.

South Herts Transport User Group

Or you can get off at Cuffley and walk the length of the Ridgeway and explore the 3 nature trails at Northaw Great Wood.

Bus 301/302/602/653 to Hatfield then Bus 341/641 weekdays or Coach 724 direct

Harpenden

An attractive traditional commuter belt town set between Luton and St. Albans, with many attractive shops, cafes, main common with cricket green and historic west common with its links golf course. Great for country walks to hatching Green, where you can lunch at the famous White Horse with its celebrated chefs. Also features the Rothampstead research centre and schools which produced many current and famous England rugby players. Now best known for its annual classic car show in late July held on the common.

Bus 321 or 357

Redbourn Common

The Cricketers is a timeless pub set on the edge of the splendid Redbourn Common with its own cricket green and now 'lunching bubbles'. Watch a cricket match in the height of summer whilst walking the common and the attractive sometimes historic houses around the edge of the exceptionally large common, or marvel at the splendour of restored historic buildings in the high street and whiling away the hours. Walk up to the historic high street on the old Roman Road, and see the former coaching inns, where coaches used to stop on journeys from London to change horses. A quiet commuter village these days but growing fast and attracting many young families with its lower house prices than St. Albans as there is no rail station.

Bus 34 weekdays.

South Herts Transport User Group

The Snow Centre, Hemel Hempstead

A newer innovation with an indoor ski centre featuring real, not synthetic snow. A great place to try out skiing and learning to ski before taking to the winter slopes in Europe and further afield. Also features facilities for younger children, snowboarding and sledging.

Bus 302.

South Herts Transport User Group

The A1 Golf Activity Centre, Rowley Lane, Barnet

A complete golf experience with new computerized golf scoring, driving range, A1 snack bar and putting greens. Easy to book and accessible from nearby Borehamwood town centre. Also features short games areas, adventure golf, indoor simulator and putting green, American golf store and tee to green coaching. Everything you need for a complete golfing experience.

Bus 601 weekdays

South Herts Transport User Group

South Herts Transport User Group

Centurion Golf and Restaurant, St. Albans

New golf complex and Michelin starred chefs in a restaurant gaining plenty of plaudits, and now hosts its own annual golf competition. The modern way to enjoy a round of golf amongst the visually stunning Prae Wood area and lakes landscape and enjoy a great meal and drink at the 19th. Now being extended to cope with demand and much sought after. Hertfordshire's best kept secret but not for long as it's fast becoming the place to golf and eat or just walk and have a drink and enjoy the ambience. Rumoured to include several top premier league players as its members?

Bus 302

South Herts Transport User Group

Go Ape, Trent Park, Cockfosters

A new attraction featuring bike trails, zip wire, high wire walkways, café, play areas and corporate training facilities. Aimed at the younger thrill seeker, but there are attractions for all ages, including just walks and a coffee for older visitors or pay areas for the very young. A stone's throw from Cockfosters' tube station, but you can feel as if you a million miles away in the treetops.

Bus 84 then TFL bus 298 or UNO 610 weekdays.

South Herts Transport User Group

St. Albans City Signal box

Located near St. Albans City Station, this period signal box has been restored to its original splendour in its original London Midland and Scottish Cream and Maroon Livery seen during its heyday of the steam era. The box is staffed by volunteers so only opens on alternate Sundays, usually between 2 and 5pm. Well worth a visit back in time, with the chance to pull some of the signal levers. Extended opening hours are available on rail and bus 'heritage' days which are advertised on their website.

Buses 84/301/302/305/601/602/724 or S1/S6/S7 to St. Albans City Station

Whipsnade Wild Animal Park

The Bedfordshire branch of the London Zoological gardens. A year round attraction for families and children alike. See the penguins, lions, tigers, rhino, giraffe, and a whole host of wild and exotic animals. A whole host of attractions and now passes available for regular visitors. A day out for all the family with other attractions and catering to make it a whole day experience. Talks about animals and special demonstrations too.

Bus 34 to Dunstable then Centre Bus 40 to Whipsnade.

Willows Activity Farm, London Colney

Everything for the family exploring the farmyard lifestyle, with farm animals, rabbits, etc. combined with soft play, tractor ides, puddle play and go kart racing. Located near London Colney, there is Peter Rabbit's Adventure playground, Mr Todd's lair, the 'big dig' sand and water play, squirrel Nutkin's treehouse, the farmyard itself and a JCB driving area.

Bus 84, 357 or 602 to London Colney.

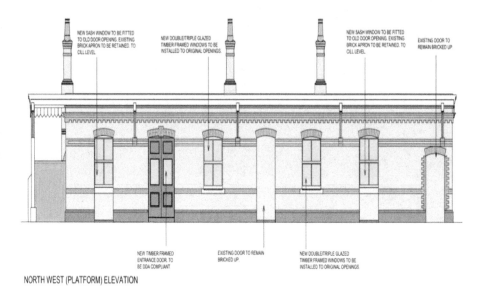

NEW SASH WINDOW TO BE FITTED TO OLD DOOR OPENING. EXISTING BRICK APRON TO BE RETAINED. TO CILL LEVEL

NEW DOUBLE/TRIPLE GLAZED TIMBER FRAMED WINDOWS TO BE INSTALLED TO ORIGINAL OPENINGS

NEW SASH WINDOW TO BE FITTED TO OLD DOOR OPENING. EXISTING BRICK APRON TO BE RETAINED. TO CILL LEVEL

EXISTING DOOR TO REMAIN BRICKED UP

NEW TIMBER FRAMED ENTRANCE DOOR. TO BE DDA COMPLIANT

EXISTING DOOR TO REMAIN BRICKED UP.

NEW DOUBLE/TRIPLE GLAZED TIMBER FRAMED WINDOWS TO BE INSTALLED TO ORIGINAL OPENINGS.

NORTH WEST (PLATFORM) ELEVATION

And a new attraction coming soon in summer 2023:

Bricket Wood Station Café and Heritage centre

A new café and heritage centre in the old re-purposed station building depicting the history of the Abbey branch line between Watford and St. Albans (and formerly Hatfield), plus the history of the Community Rail Partnership set up in 2005 and former London Country bus services in the district. Expected to open in 2022 subject to planning and other consents as this is a listed building of special interest.

Bus 361 or train to Bricket Wood station

South Herts Transport User Group

South Herts Transport User Group

River Lea and Boating centre and watercourse, Broxbourne

Part of the 2012 Olympics course and based on the River Lea and Dodds Weir picnic area, which is part of the Lea valley regional park. Many water-based activities here including boating, rowing, paddles boats or just spending time on the water on a hot day. The River and canal extend from Hertford down to Waltham Abbey so there is plenty to explore and can be accessed from many points, although Broxbourne is the main boating centre. Great fun for all ages and family days out.

Bus 301/302/602/653/724 to Hatfield then 341/641 to Broxbourne

INTENTIONALLY BLANK FOR NOTES

South Herts Transport User Group

South Herts Transport User Group

South Herts Transport User Group

South Herts Transport User Group

South Herts Transport User Group

South Herts Transport User Group

South Herts Transport User Group

97

South Herts Transport User Group

About the Author.

Paul was 64 at the time of writing this book, and married for over 30 years with 3 children, 3 grand-children and an Old English sheepdog.

Paul is a Chartered Surveyor and Engineer by training, with over 30 years' experience.

He is also a voluntary station adopter with the Abbey Line Community rail partnership since its inception in 2004/5; and has run a voluntary local transport user group since 1986.

He is also a leading UK flight and traditional archer.

Paul has written published and self-published books plus various published technical articles.

*If you enjoyed reading this book, then perhaps you may enjoy reading other titles by the same author:

Planning and Development-Changing the way we travel.

Country Bus Services after Deregulation

An Express Bus Network for Hertfordshire Business

30 Years of Bus Deregulation

My Wonderful Fran

Artificial Nocturne

@#1Crush

END

Printed in Great Britain
by Amazon